AF442429

PRAVEENA'S

BE YOU

My Beautiful!

You are Precious

Publication Note:

This book has been published in good faith that the work of the author is original. All efforts have been taken to make the material error-free. However, the author and the publisher disclaim the responsibility. No part of this book may be used, reproduced in any manner whatsoever without written permission from the author, except in the case of brief quotations embodied in critical articles and reviews.

The Book will no longer harm any gender as it is a minute scream against discrimination. It does not intend to target the entire audience as it only points out to the individuals who is biased and morally weak. This book will be a piece of cake for the people who are already literally strong and they will not have necessary to read it as they are the inspiration for this.

Dedication:

My Initial gratitude always goes to "The God almighty" who is the only reason for my every micro-macro success. My sincere thanks to, My Parents, Grandparents and my entire family. Thanks to the publications who took the role of the mother to bring out my baby book to the world beyond.

"Thanks, is the lovely word because it makes us realise that we really helped someone"

Preface

Advices are tips and shouldn't become rules henceforth. When even punished for not following it, we will not die. But hardly we are said to shadow those biased rules that exactly putting to death our life. Women are the assets of human life and it is in the hands of the social order to let the assert comfort the world. No need of boundaries for her as boundaries are framed before centuries, I gladly confirm that it due to men's incapability of protecting women. Here I would like to bring transformation in the scenario of men's feebleness of protecting women it is not women's rule to accept men's inability and ensue to be within the boundaries. Let us take the initiative to protect ourself as we already know that they have given up and accepted the inability. Enough granting chances it is our choice to decide, to look for someone to control us or to change the someone's thoughts that we are uncontrollable to do endeavours.

In this world who can precisely define or distinguish good and bad with evidence of success rate. No one it could be, as everyone is born to create their own portraits in the plain sheet of life. Do not permit or tolerate the choice of others to fill the colours as the others choice of colour for your day painting will be grey.

Acknowledgement

When writing this book, I felt like not to hurt someone individually through words or explain my hurts to get solution for the problem instead I thought to bring it out in words that would awaken people and be a lesson or at least to understand the psychologic effect of the hurt and pain of the women when they are treated in an odd way just because they are women. I acknowledge that this book will yield all the readers to a literacy world and will at least contribute for the growth of moral thoughts of all the readers.

Not Lamentations or Allegation, but might be it is,

Yes Motivation, but might be not as it is,

Might be irritating, yet you need it is,

Might not be useful, but it is,

The book you want to read is,

Here it is!

Contents

CHAPTER- 1

Working Goals

"Train your brain so that the gain rains and you shine"

Will I be a Successful Person?

Every story will have an interrogation even before it is getting started. May be like "what is the story is about?" similarly each one will have a question about her vision. It could be a doctor, teacher, engineer and many more. After achieving all these we still will have a dehydration for doing something artistic by ourself with our private inkling and finally we have hunger to twitch with our particular business and be a Boss! The Entrepreneur.

I am a female! I have strained to speech out countless things to the society where both men and women exist. As usual it nevertheless influences men it stretched to certain women and those few audiences also supported for men's emotions affirming in rapid "Men are always Men and a women cannot participate with men in all the customs". But the thing is they didn't get my point, I was not contending with men I was competing with my today to get a healthier tomorrow. That was a solution less formula that perceived subsequently from our ancestors. Still baffling but being pretended as fixed.

Women ≠ Men

The system they set are not justly the solutions but the ins and outs for their stupid rules that they conscripted in earlier centuries. Those drafts had motives that were the hollow ever, not true therefore I am not mentioning those rules here to waste your time or my paper and ink.

The elders of current generation deliberate that they sacrificed all the rules they enlisted for women henceforth the women are getting rationalized, nevertheless the truth is "Women were, are and will grieve, ever and ever... equally physically and mentally". Those rubrics were mounted to upset women and to place her further down men's foot. Afterward bearing all the agony with smile and silence she is still entitled to be a weaker sex.

How brainy these strategies are **"killing emotions in silence is also a violence"** Numerous men have their voice louder by drafting duplicate case files in contradiction of female's innocence for no reason. Why are we weaker sex? For the capability that we had to follow all unwise rules or for the inability that we didn't have to upsurge against you to slap and express that your rules are stupid as you!

How fools' women are "The man ponders", As Women were thought to be too good and kind which paved way for the independence of being bad, arrogant and dominant in men comparatively.

Women's reaction for every accusation be like "I haven't done any mistake but I was forcefully thought to be fearful always, But why? Because I am a Women?"

I really feel bad that I am not crafty to express all regrets of women's as I couldn't get adequate alphabets; I can't afford such massive number of papers. If trees were able to hear they will shed papers as an alternative of leaves to aid me carve about women's sorrow. Millions of Victims, Oodles of lives disappeared without living a satisfactory life due to the motive of men's shit pleasure.

Our peace into pieces and those pieces became a solution less riddle.

Sure, it is a ruthless immeasurable pressure for their pleasure.

The accomplishment of the womankind lies the future of the world. To recite this frequently is the fundamental concern of all the influencers and I sense gratified to be in that list of those Millions who had formerly gave voice for Women empowerment since several eras. They might have felt that they have made deviations for the forthcoming peers and there would be no Male command or Old-style attack to the Women in the impending years nevertheless the thing is, once the erroneous moral is rooted as a seed it is the accountability of the care taker to make the tree fertile without toxic substance diffusion over it. When the care taker rests caring, the toxins in the root will o'er supper the trees and lead to be hazardous for the entire tree. Me as a writer and a few as parents, educators and few others as politicians will have to elevate voice up until the root is detached away and implanted with the hale and hearty seed.

Bearing in mind all the injustice there were various virtue people functioned and still operates for Women's welfare. When a lady becomes a chief in the society, she will turn out to be a ruler an educated head, an entrepreneur!

The deed of women can be sturdier once she grows into an entrepreneur

Female Entrepreneurs are still deficient in numbers and they cannot be recognised identical to men at any cause. The World is progressive with equality and freedom, for women is approved so much, says many then, why is the topmost richest people in the world are only men and not women. I didn't take a stretch to research on it for the reason that I can say it certainly that not one woman in that list is in topmost richest people in the world. What could be the cause in arrears? Do we have explanation or can we settle it with the saying "Black Magic"?

The realism behind this is women are approved with quantified opportunity to work then what will be the leeway for them to be a boss?

World Economic Forum states that "Women are seen as better coders than men-but only if they hide their gender"

That is the exact proud moment for Men. Men are paying less for women and exploitation of all female talents, hard work are happening to earn out of it, this statement neither false nor can be disagreed with statistics that shows women's growth rate. Few never let women to enter the race, few let them inside and tease them, few let them run the race and push them down and few let them to run the race but no one will let them finish the race it could be from anywhere from anybody. Here I don't say those obstacles are only men it could also be the elder women from their family, their own cousin and their surroundings as a whole. In spite of all these hurdles I always would like to highlight men as the major villain because if men think women can lead. Every Husband should support wife, every brother should support her sister and stand by her to speak out for her rights. No compromise can be done from our side here after let those decades when women were called as the individuals of sacrificing and compromising their wishes and ambition come to an end. Why compromise for whom they should compromise and for what substitution they should compromise. One life with very little life span why to compromise who should have rights on one's personal wish and thirst for accomplishment or to enjoy and to Rome around is one's own choice.

We strictly restrict your restrictions here after

No need of advises as we have six senses

No greedy words needed to feed us to stop our success

We can be blamed after a mistake happens but not before we set off something with Interest

Actually, I find people lazy all the days except when they come for advising unnecessary stuff to prove that they were not lazy but were actually thinking for our future all the time and that is the achievement of them and they call it experience

Experience occurs when we try something and learn from it but before trying you stop us and conclude that "It won't work out"

How is it possible to envisage future even before knowing about what you are going to predict. Are you an Alien from future, Ancestors from past, Nostradamus or Astrologer.

Alright women knew nothing you say! I agree for false. If so, accepting this way, will you let us to learn something! Absolutely 'No', we women are said to hear that is open only our ears and to keep the mouth shut.

Remembered the three wise monkeys!

See no evil

Hear no Evil

Speak no Evil

Women here are Foolish monkeys!

See no one eye to eye

Speak no opinion

Hear, nod but react deaf

Those monkeys lead a better life than women, I guess…

Here, I halt speaking about those people who downturn women. I
didn't want to tribute all women and blame all men. Because I find
countless women being the rival of women due to existence jealous,
domination in terms of age, education, status, caste and religion. It is
those women bounces authority for men to dominate another woman.
It might be a mother who teaches her son to yield control over his wife
or a mother-in-law who corners her daughter in law for not doing all
the household works individually on time and the list is endless with
the accusation. The motive behind bringing a girl into one's family is to
let her live her life better than her previous days but not to brand your
present comfortable by governing, advising and treating her as a
slave. So, I will not throw my arrows towards men alone for every
woman's emotional attack. I would like to make a guilt attack to each
mother who thought her son with old banned custom of overpowering

women which was accepted those days and made to accept forcefully. But it will not be suitable or acceptable today as women are equally educated, working, most wanted for economic growth of the country and women are equally brave. When I had discussions with my friends after their marriage, I was able to acknowledge that the old dominating rules are still existing in all of our life. Primarily we had tears when discussing things but we later on track laughed at those because we realised that we ignored all stuffs and stayed away. This book is for all the women and dreamers who needs motivation to accomplish their career paths.

Animals with five senses are gifted to live with freedom to live their life and there is no animal opposing the opposite gender.

Lion is called as the King of the forest by Human yet we all recognize that the Lion is the laziest animal and Lioness is the actual king. If I have had the opportunity to talk to the animals directly and recognize their language, they would be glad to accept that the Lioness is the King of the forest and not the Lion. I express gratitude to God as they don't recognize human language and I sense that is the reason that they live fortunately as identical as always. The day they come to know about dominating the gender then the destruction contribution of the earth will commence from their side as well. Man slayed Animals to become safer, man cut downs all the trees to turn out to be rich, correspondingly man controls women to be more comfortable. From these we come to know man might not have had growth without destruction of other creatures. Being super comfortable and reaching heights cannot be well-thought-out as the accomplishment whereas the physical, mental and social pressures are being handled by the women on one side and struggle, a girl undergoes every day to work for her goal is the ultimate discomfort that male cannot grip even for a day. Among all these muddles she wins and she is the Woman and I am roaring my motivating voice for her.

Lion is less than lioness as looking ferocious alone cannot overtake the reality.

Motivation is like seeds that spill in to wealthy land therefore I assure you that after reading this book all your wealthy thoughts, ideas will emerge and give a fruitful feat in life. I had massive motivation from my family during my teens but subsequently becoming a woman we will not get any motivation because we are parted away from our parents. I have to pursuit my own motivation and I thru all my self-motivation as words and it turned out to be a book.

CHAPTER -2

Women's Career

Career can have arrears

repeat, progress and prove!

A man shorn of Occupation is not well-thought-out as Man but then in attendance no such statements we have for women. This is the time to spell a slogan for women.

Worthy not, you women without a Work life and dreams!

A woman partakes two choices, to drive back to the past and give birth to many Children or to go to the forthcoming days to give secured life to the Children, family, funding surroundings, economy, and to create an ocean space for women in the world.

To give Birth or to give life it depends on the choices that a woman chooses. The Truth is that, she can give the both.

Build your career in spite of all muddles. Turn out to be superior to men, this time it is going to be our turn, as women can control men in a right way. On no account restrictions in the future for women will occur for directing men because this time the authority with be with us completely. I am damn sure that a man who admires, tolerates and smiles at the dominating women are certainly Manly. Because he feels proud for her growth, without any fear of the consequences he can show green flag to all the verdicts she makes. A Man becomes fearless to Women's actions when he has confidence in himself, in his strength, in his mental fitness that he can bounce at all opportunity for her picks and support her without difficulty all through her catastrophes.

Occupation is the subject strength for women but constructing an own empire as an entrepreneur is still conceivable. It could be a small scale or large-scale, women can make it probable to be an entrepreneur even by being an individual person. For example, she could be a baker, a chef, a software developer, Animator, a Costume Designer or anything.

Anything she can be, be it anything or say it anything she will do it in a go- The Women.

Becoming an entrepreneur is a herculean task because of the determination she lays on the job and in spite of all society barriers as arrows that are thrown in several ways for girls. For example, Men endure Caste discrimination where as women undergo equally Caste discrimination and gender discrimination. And yet again, when Men go through religious discernment, women experience religious perspicacity as well as forced to shadow cultural outdated values that could affect their mental health, upsurge anxiety and also get their rights of self-deciding elementary things such as dress code, education, career, life partner, subsequently after marriage yet again a certain prolonged tilt of rules and protocols. As an outcome, the society faults women for not being super picture-perfect yet if she is trying to be super perfect there is no appreciation given voluntarily.

Women entail appreciation out of thirst but the remarks she receives is "it is just her duty, humdrum and there is nothing more distinct about it to applaud". Truly, subsequently going through these lists woman set aside her time, money, harvest ideas, stands alone and starts her professional life. It is mandatory for every selfless woman to be highly praised not only for the sake of motivating them but also for the things that they are already going through.

I observed at this list for a while and all and sundry need to have a look at it habitually, every month, every year for the own good of motivation. This list is from October 2022!

1.   **Elon Musk**
2.   **Jeff Bezos**
3.   **Bernard Arnault**
4.   **Bill Gates**
5.   **Warren Buffett**
6.   **Larry Page**
7.   **Sergey Brin**
8.   **Larry Ellison**
9.   **Steve Ballmer**
   10. Mukesh Ambani

I frequently look up to the topmost ironic personalities in the world like them and admire, I was indeed longing for some women to remain in the top of the list and I came across a few women ranked underneath possessed businesses connected to Cosmetics, food and Cloths on the other side subsequently I observed into Men's occupational lists, they already roofed all the sectors in the world. This thru me think how the Women Entrepreneurs Notions had ascended starved of any complications, for the reason that their key target audience were Women and the concepts of business were based on Women's psychology.

We Women are not only destined for owning Cosmetics, Selling Cloths or Food, but there is some degree *to work out there, to work now more, to work more to rule, to rule to get the right place, to get the place is the actual place where we show us to the men and the society where we should be kept actually.*

"Pass your goals possibly soon without taking a Pause Please"

Our World is a Woman, so as Woman is a World, there is no discrepancy between both the powers. I am not a feminist; I tribute the women with motto and I presage the individuals who sojourns their motto and extinguishes the inner peace. The warning is applicable for the society with male and female in common. I warrant to recurrence this over that I don't support all women. It is predominantly for women who yells for their self-respect, self-independence, self-love, self-emotions and about their every self, because they are actually targeted by the society that never cares about anybody rather than to show off the fake dominations.

I would wish to see enlarged number of the Women Entrepreneurs in the forthcoming days and I start lettering some strategies that I can bounce with my instincts.

According to me, I bid to define "Entrepreneur is the one who conquests the heart of the consumers and likewise grosses smart profit out of it. It necessitates nourishing of consumer desires, benefits and pleasure. In order to attain all things, one must have the capacity to work as an all-rounder. Hence as an entrepreneur she is the Task bearer and risk taker who achieves the infinite targets and work for her goals".

A Woman is a wonderful resource!

Entrepreneurship is an art of manufacture profit out of any available resources in order to gain satisfaction. Here women are actually egg headed to make something boundless with the accessible few things. A woman might be considered as full of emptiness for many but she is a creator of human. Yes, women are itemized as weedy, poor soul, uncapable, dependent, physically weak and useless in general when equated to men in many places but in reality, when she perhaps crops a living human resource indeed which styles the world population with the god's boon then what not she can do to achieve. There might be some snags in attaining entrepreneurship due to various reasons. But still the Entrepreneur makes a target to achieve her business goals.

CHAPTER-3

Goals of Entrepreneur

"No goal in life; go foul in life"

Goal is an obligatory stuff looked-for all individual's triumph. For women it is dual thought-provoking entity.

One life is her life, her choice and her decision. Don't continually stab to display the supremacy you have over status, age, gender, racism and experience. Don't put on your silly wishes, the framed responsibilities to her she is not born for satisfying your expectations. And don't ever call her feminist, arrogant, insolent or with any depraved words that labels her physical appearance. Look, she has her own sixth sense and knows to do what she desires to do. So don't play smart associating her with other girls. Every girl is unique and she is jam-packed of goals and dreams. Being a slice of society, the negative vibes is being fenced by her while she is trying to survey rigidly in the path of thorns and fire. But on one occasion she is done in accomplishing her success, they arise forward-facing before her to take the credits as if they supported her from root. How silly it sounds! After all the women still remains silent with tears and gratified smile after she completes her goal

Hey women! You are merely a football rolling on the ground being kicked thrown to reach the goal. You will be scared when thrown, you will be hurt when kicked, you will grasp the goal and win the trophy of freedom finally one day where you get supremacy to teach a lesson based on what you have gone through.

Preaching to reach goal is so easy as I do. But to do it, after saying "stop it" is what I mean it, the sad it is for the women to let it, go as it is ordered by someone who framed it.

Goal is the significant factor of attainment both in business and personal life. An entrepreneur requires bull's eye to accomplish her services in various sectors. She cannot achieve it without certain goals and principles. Each and every entrepreneur has a unique strategy and pathway to complete the target so called her success. An entrepreneur's mark hinge on the estimated poise and capacity to achieve it. Henceforth the target fluctuates based on every individual's capacity. The stipulation of the entrepreneur is merely based on the policies that she has in the course of the business idea, the plan that she has to shadow the idea and implementation of the plan is the chief role of the entrepreneur. Hence it is vibrant that qualification does not comprise of education or status it primarily deals with the psychological work done by the entrepreneur in order to charm both the consumers and the employees.

Entrepreneur appeals consumers by means of marketing the products or the services in innumerable customs and on the other hand the employees also get driven due to upsurge profit level and thus will further lead to the progress of the company. The expansion of the company will apparently result in alteration in lifestyle of the employees. This is due to intensification in income out of profit.

Instead of chasing human satisfaction as an ordinary woman she can chase the customer satisfaction as an extraordinary entrepreneur

Importance of Entrepreneurship

Entrepreneurship has various important features as follows;

Increased Entrepreneurship will lead to decreased exploitation of human work, as everyone turn out to be a boss of their own world one day.

1. Ability to rally the standard of living and generate wealth that helps for the development of the economy.

2. It helps to get-up-and-go change in the mode of thinking, approach and to pact with the situation in a pioneering way.

3. It empowers to progress novel markets and makes mobility laid-back.

4. Entrepreneurship primes to creation of job opportunities and thus diminishes unemployment. Thus, it helps to condense the struggle faced by the individuals in the economy.

5. An Entrepreneur who is the reason behind entrepreneurship is the action taker and also a highly self-motivated one who thinks day and night for the victory of the business.

6. The perception of an entrepreneur acts as a mile stone for her success. If the entrepreneur's perception is right, she then can make a good entrepreneurship and proceed.

7. Entrepreneurship leads to growth of civilization and plays a major role in social welfare.

8. The expansion of whole economy deceits on the goalmouths of entrepreneurship. Thus, it makes deviations in the infrastructure and geographical changes as well.

9. Promotes research and development which aids to ease scientific growth of the economy.

10. It creates various influences on the community development that pledges many positive properties in the society.

11. Creates political and economic amalgamation between the countries.

Role of an Entrepreneur:

"Profit or Loss be a Pro to fit in to it to conclude it as Profit"

Entrepreneur dream dollars before they make an idea. They are termed as "Risk bearers and success hunters". A risk bearer is the one who is able to face both profit and loss and proceed further. Entrepreneur has the skill to deal with perilous situations and also have solutions for all the barriers that are yet to come when the risk turned out to be an issue. The entrepreneur is gifted to contemplate about the future is her major perception skill. On the other hand, the entrepreneur is a feat stalker. Her risk bearing aptitude will lead to triumph and thus she demonstrates to be an efficacious entrepreneur. They are the big bold examples of an economically established society. The key role laid by them contributes a lot to the economic development. Entrepreneur's moral achievement is chiefly accomplished when she fulfils the need of the people with her key ideas.

"Never knows to say NO to one's own ideas even if it tends to be a super risky one"

Thus, the entrepreneur styles a good idea, decision, plan and action. These four steps help the entrepreneur to implement her task properly. When there is a lag in any of these steps then the entrepreneur has to face it.

Idea Generation: Idea can be modest but the route to root those ideas to the world as a splendid one with the aid of marketing is the real Idea behind every idea.

Ideas changes lives. The invention and innovation started with the idea. The experience that one possesses leads to alternative thinking. The options are created when we over think something and apply it for a purpose. The corrections are further made with experience. After all the analysis made out of experience resulted in alternative thinking and gave rise to options. The options created analysis and after the analysis the idea is generated for a specific purpose. Ideas are the fallouts of trial and error that are thru by us and our competitors formerly. The extra we toil on understanding the impossibility will give us the possible and acceptable idea.

Decision Making: The better idea can be instigated only when we style a right pronouncement at the right time. Decision making is not an easy chore. It acts as a root cause for every beginning. Ideas may come first but decision acts as the preliminary phase of any process because each decision that we make can have two possibilities. "To proceed with the go or to stop and drop"

The least chance given to the girls were in decision making, they cannot brand their own decision and I sense that this could be the reason that the world is still towards the rear. As we all distinguish the customers or consumers in both the gender but the ideas, decision is thru by men earlier and that is the reason that the world is unfeeling, robotic and machinelike without any emotions, colours and in conclusion the evolution befallen only in technologies and gadgets as a replacement for of food, life, nature and other colourful things. Remember if women might have taken charge over the food industry there would have been no leeway for Junk foods, processed food coming int the business which intended at taste and money instead of health and satisfaction. Have you ever thought about this beforehand? I can guarantee that if the world had most female business people in niche, then just visualize the world, it could have been with too many thought-provoking real time entertainments that will make every individual to be more childish, innocent and emotional. But when this perhaps being tumble-down without open-handed opportunities for women to elect on big things then the world becomes Machine and the humans too. Innocence slayed, Emotions concealed, Money and comfort to be lazy augmented progressively.

Planning: Once the decision is made a plan should be designed in order to make the further action. Planning plays a major role in any type of work. Without a plan no action can be performed. Many projects went disastrous deprived of planning; countless women are suffering without proper planning. A women can perhaps plan about expenses of monthly income, savings for the family. But there is something much more she can fix to use her planning skills for the progress of the society. She can plan to accomplish her wishes and ambition; she can plan to work on it by doing substitute arrangements with her regular routine but as of our situation is concerned a woman is planning a lot to express her fortitude or goal to her family and get approval to work on it knowing it earlier that it is going to be forbidden and will be at a standstill. This is the eventual planning that she is permitted to make. Just imagine if the women take so much of time in getting approval and convincing the surroundings to work on her ambition, after too much of opposition both dominantly and emotionally, think of how exhausted she will be while starting to work on it. In this mental exhaustion she gambols her plans and there her life ends but she is just alive without a purpose.

Plan to overhaul all further plans to make any process complete its purpose.

Action: This is the eventual phase of the progression where the accomplishment takes place. For every action there involves many considerations that includes Time management, Punctuality, Awareness about the Competition, Control over the procedure and process, Implementation of plan and follow up with the action. These components contribute a lot in achieving the target action. Once the action is executed appropriately the success will go easy. Women are much more skilled with this as many schedules in the day today life are carried out by them. Even if the decision, plans are taken by men, the action is taken by women indirectly where they are assigned with a lot of works to make the actions possible without gaining any recognition. The actions are performed by women with the ascendency of men who necessitates the final credits and financial paybacks for his comfort.

These four steps contribute a lot for deed. It is not only for entrepreneurs but also for every work we are tangled with in our day today life. Hence it is not a theoretical idea for entrepreneur's goal. It acts as the real-world progression for all the work and routines.

"The chance that was once over was not actually over... It is a beginning "

Entrepreneur uses every plausible chance for her success. There is no end of opportunities for entrepreneurs. Because Entrepreneur is sage enough to make use of every opportunity and finds profit out of it. Opportunity is the tool that is used to make Success for every entrepreneur. A virtuous use of opportunity at the precise time may result in many changes in the acuity and action. An amplified opportunity grants dual success. Hence no prospect is wasted by the entrepreneur.

Forces that drive Entrepreneurship:

The forces are the optimistic thoughts that come mainly out of drive of ambition or achievement. It can be emerged due to various reasons that initiate or entice the entrepreneur with the idea which leads them to make accomplishment out of it, there are various forces that may encourage the entrepreneurs which includes;

Rivalry

"It is incomplete or empty when you reached something without any competition"

Rivalry makes intrants and therefore the competitors lead the consumers or consumers to utterly new market spaces, forcing the companies to spend greater amounts on product development. There are also many hostile competitors who do any type of task with numerous approaches to mimic anything ground-breaking or new to attempt by the company. She is making it tougher and firmer to bring out the unique frame of the companies. Here the other competitors face innumerable brawls with the aggressiveness of the specific competitors but however she might be violent in the point of competitors but she is always a high-flier in view of the customers. Companies find themselves competing with companies in other industries that play by completing different rubrics and protocols making contemporary competitive approaches extraneous. Rubrics and protocols make changes in the achievement side of the companies. Some companies provide independence to work and some companies may have several politics rules and targets to achieve. Women are meant to handle politics each and every day even within the family. The politics that transpire within the family is even worse than the professional side as we might not have any emotional attachment with the professional life, we will not get hurt with the politics that transpires within the company but when it originates in family it is still problematic understand about it and the profit that they gain out of it.

When considering both the views companies with rules achieve faster. Therefore, rules and regulations also act as one of the competition factors. The Competitors are also being specialized in following narrow track which attempts profitable niches. They evade cost of competing across a broader product and consumer range, while attacking the company's most money-making areas of business. Therefore, every step of the competitor bouts another competitor. However, one faces lose due to competition.

Clients

"The buyer is the actual giver for an entrepreneur"

The clients are the authentic target of each and every entrepreneur. The consumer is equal to profit. The consumer can also be stated as buyer, purchaser, client and so on. But for an entrepreneur consumer is called as profit or income source. The consumers come from the group of audience who had some idea about purchasing a product. The consumer becomes a user once after using the product. The user turns out to be a consistent consumer when she is gratified with the particular product. On the other hand, if the consumer quests for another brand of the same product, it is apparent that the consumer is disgruntled with the product. This might become forfeiture for the company. One patron's satisfaction can increase the number of users where as one dissatisfied consumer can stop many buyers from purchasing a product.

Nowadays the customer's anticipation force towards the companies is hastily increasing. The companies customize their products, customer, support function and communication approaches and yet have many ways to do so in order to preserve standards of the company. The way of communication that the company have towards the consumers will upshot in long-term consumer relationships. This way of approach from the company exhibits the sustainable skills that they possess towards maintaining their treasured customers. Sustainable growth is maintained by implementing new skills in serving global markets. Women are known for their excellent sales skills so that they attract buyers of various industry. The Sales skill is comprehensive when there is extreme patient, toleration, observation, convincing skills. Marketing skills etc... Therefore, this pitch can also be jam-packed by women in the upcoming days completely.

Ethical standards

"Standard exhibits the withstanding art of the company"

The company's standard starts with the eminence of the product. The consumers create brand based on the standard of the product. If the quality of the product is upright the consumer himself generates brand name for the particular product by word of mouth or suggesting the product to the new user. Hence the company need not create its own brand by outlaying too much on advertising or marketing.

The term Ethical standard describes the moral philosophy mounted for maintaining the standard. It means the company should preserve standard through permissible rules and regulations. The evidence of the quality and standards should be morally applied and demonstrated with records. Companies are progressively liable to many of the stakeholders and their activities are more visible in forcing management to make hard-hitting choices and carry results while behaving with responsibility. More lawsuits upsurge company cost and castigate innovative actions. Regulatory of restrictions perimeter, the innovative choices and ideas while obliging companies to cram new ways to vie with each other.

CHAPTER-4

Time Management

"Past cannot be brought back

But future can solve anything that lacks..."

Time is all we need in life. It is unstoppable when going and unchangeable when it is over. Many movies have come and many scientists have exasperated to bring back time by the idea of time machine. The funniest thing in this is that they knew it is impossible to bring back the time but still they want it and they crack for it. Here we can come to know about their over confidence to formulate the time machine, Idiocy of their over confidence and the most vital thing is the gluttony that they have in changing the past for some lucrative reason. I have noticed one more thing here, that is nothing but they still waste their time discerning about their past. They decay their present and future by concentrating on past. One need not contemplate to change the time or incidents that happened already if the whole shebang happened to be good. It is our state of mindfulness that helps to make everything stable and good. Time can be made into sweet memories when we use it fruitfully. Hence it is very important to utilise the time properly by initiating time management ideas.

"Time Management" is the technique of organizing and planning by which we spend our time on precise goings-on. It is the counterintuitive to dedicate precious time to learn about time and to style action out of it. Time management aids to accomplish any type of task in a petite period which fallouts in gaining a lot of free time. It also leads to gaining of learning opportunities, to reduce the stress level and helps to emphasis on the next work simultaneously. Each and every work that are focused and completed with the time management stretches the best experience to the next work. Hence application of time management at work helps to save time and learn the risk bearing skills. Time management is simply stated in one word that it is the "conscious control of time" to do a task successfully.

Time Management for people in Career

"Eat the ice cream before it melts

Wait for the meat to cook"

To be fast or to wait depends on the work you choose!

At the present time there is no far difference between career and future, they are very interrelated. When one has a good career automatically her future turns out to be good. To reach pinnacle one must take part in rivalry with the world. Time management is the key or initial tool to take part in any type of rivalry. Time is actually a term that deals with mathematics. Time can be calculated and tasks can be scheduled accordingly. But the value of time cannot be premeditated.

There is no formula or measuring tool to gage the worth of time. The value of time can only be sensed it pacts with human emotions and behaviour. When we cram to measure the value of time by ourselves, we can gain lot of experience and develop various skills of management. Time management and career are like the two sides of the same coin. When one does her assigned work on time, she is gifted fit in to her career so well. A career builder will focus on the most significant task and cultivate her acquaintance to work for it. she concocts a list of work with the specific order. Thereby she breaks the task in to smaller pieces to make it easy to do. Later she thinks about the break that she can avail during the task. Here the break does not mean that she is in need of rest. The break is allotted to check the output of the previous task. But overall, she achieves her work on time and there lies her real success. Thus, to make a schedule of success one needs to deal with time management.

Time Management for Students

"The art of creativity in time management was initially started with the student"

An upright learner is initially quantified as a student. In this globe everyone plays a role of a learner and a teacher. Thus, everyone is apparently Student again. Students at present-day will be the imminent of the nation. Students are the seamless ones who make time schedules to study their daily lessons and complete their projects and assignment. Mostly students make a good time schedule but very few follow the schedules and achieve. Students are very much capable of creating short cut ideas to achieve their task. The indolence that the students have also creates some time management skills and built creativity in them. Creativity comes from students. Normally if the time schedule is made for an hour students can complete that same task within 30-40 minutes. It might be due to their creativity implementation or laziness to do the task step by step that results in search of shortcuts and the unity that they have in making the short cut ideas. This is because the students prioritize their time to be spent on entertainment, games and fun so that they do not prefer to spend much time on other essential task that helps them to grow and shine. In such cases there are also exceptional students who spend more than the anticipated time to do a task. And those students show off their maximum interest in that particular task. The output that they give out of it will always be unique and the time that they have spent for it remains fruitful. Those exceptional students are really the future of our nation. The initial thing that every successful student sacrifice in her life is the valuable time. She sacrifices the entertainment, fun and so many things in her life. But on the other hand, she used her time so well and in her the key of time management exists. Time management is not the subject that the student erudite, it is the practical knowledge that the learner acquired out of experience and applies it in her day today life unconsciously in many ways. When the learner thinks it seriously and become conscious about time management then she is no more a learner. she will become the advisor or teacher who makes others to be aware of time and its sources.

Tips for Time management

"Tips are just advices unless and until it is applied"

Tips come out of good and bad experiences confronted by the people. The distribution of opinion or experience does not reach so many ears whereas giving some guidelines and advices are being well-thought-out by the people. Hence for constructing it extra beneficial I would like to include various tips for time management and they are as follows;

1.   **To distinguish your time:**

Primarily start finding out how you devote your whole day. Learn to track the work done and time disbursed on the work daily. Make a record of the work done and make some corrections out of it. The alterations may comprise discovering the likelihood of dipping the time of work, finding the areas to expand and so on.

2.   **Before Starting determine your desired result:**

You must have the clear inkling of what you do and the resolution of why you do. Creating an agenda will lessen the wastage of time and the work is done almost on time.

3.   **Make a firm time limit on each task:**

Have a look at the agenda and detect the task that takes longer time than you expect. By setting time constraints for those activities, you will focus more and work more resourcefully on it. If you still find it difficult to find yourself going beyond the time limit, examine your workflow and eliminate little time-wasters like unscheduled breaks.

4.   Make a special plan for Sunday:

The work that is done on Sunday is to some degree special because it is the resting day for all. The curiosity in the direction of the work will on no occasion let you take rest and on the other hand the work done on Sunday goes so horizontal without pressure. I would like to give a real time example here: I started writing this book on a good Sunday and finished it on another good Sunday.

5.   Create a daily plan:

Daily plan is a mandatory thing to be applied and followed by the target individual. When one decides to achieve the target, she goes with the flow of daily plan. Following the plan may be difficult at all the times but still the target individual will have control over the plan and achieves her goal.

6.   Make a table of DONE and TO DO task:

Sometimes the task that you do may have to be repeated again and again. This parting of work done and work to do task will help you to divide your work accordingly and work towards it. It can be anyway such as work done in previous week and work to be done in the next week or else work done yesterday and work to be done tomorrow. The "work done" column acts as the motivation factor of an individual. It reminds the individual about the accomplishments she made earlier and acts as the push factor to complete the task on time.

7.   Complete the demanding task first:

The work cannot be done in a given order and it will not be applicable for every situation. It is important to choose the task according to its time consumption. Some may prefer to do the difficult task initially and easier task at the last. It can be vice versa as well. The priority for choosing the work depends on the demand of the buyer. For example: When there is a demand for biscuits the company need not concentrate on the flavours of the biscuits. Its main objective should be distribution of biscuits to the buyers on time.

8.   Evade all the commotions:

Any type of work at any time will have some distractions and diversions. Nowadays the main commotion for everybody is the mobile phones. Most of us spend our majority of time by chit chat, watching videos just with the purpose to waste the time. Apart from mobile phones there are numerous distractions so called temptations. It could be wandering around with friends and family or worsening of time due to sluggishness act as the severe and unexpected distraction for an individual leads to health issues.

"Owning limited Sources of access to fun will wall against distractions"

As limited Internet at higher charge were used lucratively and unlimited Internet at Economical charge is being used uselessly"

9.   Do not try multitasking all the time:

Doing more than a few activities at a time is thought-provoking and also stimulating. But it may root some thoughtless blunders in between. Multitasking is indeed a virtuous skill but still it is not applicable at all the occasions. Multitasking can save time and boost the productivity but one who is adept with multitasking skills can be able to do certain task. But still there are sophisticated jeopardy of doing multitasking which can cause boo-boos and mistakes. Finding the errors will again lead to lack of time. Hence it is better to avoid multitasking while dealing with risky task.

10. Do not pause for opportunities to knock the door:

"If not NOW then HOW?"

Waiting can be done is some cases but it is not meant to be at rest until the opportunity knocks the door. Waiting for your turn certainly means the fortitude that you need to have towards the accomplishment of the chore and not for the idleness that you have till the opportunity comes to your place. May be late the chance comes we ought to be prepared to drive through it anytime. Hence it is very much needed to be imperatively prepared earlier with the sport shoes, Jersey and rain coat to run a race in a cold lazy winter rain. Actually, it tends to be relaxed to work if you jolt working on a winter because the world is indolent waiting for the summer whereas for you the summer had already started when you have decided to be curt.

"If started in Winter, you can beat Ant's Success"

11.   Do not strive for perfection:

"Perfection does not exist anywhere it depends on the feedback"

Do not get frighten for making your work flawless or by trying to please others. When everything wants to be seamless it needs lot of suggestions and feedback. Considering each and every feedback and working on it will generate tautness, Anxiety, pain and heaviness will halt the flow of work. Hence it is much healthier to go with one's own style and thought so that it will at least generate rightness and satisfaction to own self.

12. Plan a pause between the responsibilities:

Break may not be well-thought-out to be an imperative part of any work but still one needs disruption to contemplate and continue her work. Use those pause time for connecting with the universe that gave your life, Thanksgiving to the Universe Creator and to feel regretful for Nature Every day. This break will upsurge the determination of living and progress your emotions towards Triumph.

13. Unify your effort:

The chief way of conquest or work lies on the way of organizing it. The organizing skill needs a lot of involvement and practice. A greenhorn cannot encompass in establishing an event. Organizing skills twitches from small activities and then step by step it is applied in superior task and thus it is applicable in work place.

14. Coach your other side of the brain to work:

The other part of the brain means the other activities that you get encaged with and not the Professional side of you. It may comprise of engaging in hobbies and concentrating on other interest of yours. It may be any sports or physical activities such as jogging or gym work out and so on. Here the significant skills secreted privately are being exhibited and creativity is becoming advanced in you.

15.   A good sleep and exercises can boost your work span:

"Sleep is the main source of action where new ideas are born"

It might be unbelievable for many to admit that ideas come while partaking a deep thinking in sleep. Sleep is the only source of relaxation. Sleeping on time and waking up on time encompasses time management. Too much of sleep can also cause weariness and idleness which will touch other schedules as well. Hence sleep or rest at regular intervals is essential factor of every individual.

"Power nap showers you with sure ideas"

16.   Make custom of the Calendar:
A Calendar is a good source of scheduling tool or reminder to plan any event. Without calendar there is no scheduling. Usage of diary emerged and increased day by day because diary is linked with calendar. Not only business professionals but also the students, teachers and all other professional individual entail calendar to schedule their forthcoming works and also to go through the work done prior. It acts as one's own record of the activities done therefore Time management and Calendar are interconnected.

"No End to Calendar so as your as your Success if you Schedule and work on it"

17.   Spend some time for Slackening:

The time that you devote unaccompanied at a quiet place will help your brain work faster and acts as the energy saver for supplementary thinking. One surprise thing about quiet time is that it certainly fills us with the optimistic sensations. Individual who has the monotonous habit of doing meditation turn out to be psychologically sturdy. Those personalities rally their ability of being enduring and also precision in subsequent routine healthy habit without anybody commencement. Spending some time for relaxation is fine whereas taking too much of rest will result in sluggishness and incompleteness.

"The only reason behind every relaxation should be to proceed further"

18.   Say No to all the Obstacles:

Interferences are the part of every single task we do in our day today life. However, we try to evade all the impediments intensely, it will still continue with us through any of the sources in the surroundings. It is in our hands to deal with all those futile obstacles and say no to it. If we contemplate those annoying obstacles seriously and get side-tracked on our regular routine, our success plot will get pretentious. Hence, we will not be able to reach the task destination on time. Saying "NO' to all the impediments will bound us with some positive spirit to progress fast and accomplish. We must take the deadly obstacles as a drive to do the task in a haste with perfection. Thus, sidestepping unwanted stuff saves your treasured time.

"May be said every obstacle grant strength, funnily not you lose all strength in tolerance"

19.   Make it early to finish:

Being Punctual gives the first impression to anybody. Carrying out the work on time is not an optional thing it is very compulsory to do the given work on or before the given time. Lag at work will disturb the others time as well. One must understand that wasting one's own time is okay but we have no authority to make others wait and waste their time. Hence it is very essential to do the task on time or prior. It is very hard to be punctual but once you adept to be you are already on the track of victory.

"On time is all Success"

20.   Follow up with the yield and make final analysis:

The final pace of every mission is to follow up with the work done and compare the productivity with the competitors. Look into your role done and analyse the slip-ups in it so that it will not be repeated further. The ability to distinguish our capacity through the criticism collected about the work. This is the concluding step of any task and should be taken utterly than the other steps. Because once the work is completed it automatically becomes as a part of our past experiences which will guide us for our supplementary works. Hence it is mandatory to analyse every work after it is completely done.

"Work done is already over and categorised as a past experience that helps us to be super conscious with the further works"

These are some of the major tips that are to be followed up with time management. Initiate these into your thoughts and start working on it by implementing all these views.

CHAPTER-5

Wake up

"It's Alarm's Sound"

"Every ringing alarm before sunrise is the singing song for your success"

Alarm is just a part of cue. But now I contemplate Alarm as the main subject that is accompanying towards one's perfection, psychology, behaviour, planning, ideology so on... Here we have made some perceptions having the concept of Alarm. It is not the proof that I stretch out of each case, it is completely opinionated.

Initiative of Mrs. A

Ms. A drives to bed at 12.00 PM and she sets alarm for 4.00 AM on the next day. It is almost 12.00 PM when she is off to sleep. Is it perhaps possible for her to wake up at 4.00 AM in the next morning? Does she have at all work to wake up this early at 4.00 AM?

Let us grasp what happened on the next day. The next day it was super quiet at 3.59 AM and it is getting closer and about to hit four. The alarm sound is head to foot deafening. It was as flashy as a cry of a baby. The sound did not bring the definite feeling of an alarm instead it just gave severe irritation to Ms. A. This is because she napped so late yesterday and she never wants to get up early responding to the alarm. Then why did she set her alarm in the previous day? The reason behind every alarm is just a small initiative that she takes every day to get up early and execute some work. Yes, this is not the first day she sets alarm, this is being repeated daily. Here Ms. A just wishes to take initiative to get up early in the morning. Here we can analyse to distinguish that Ms. A just wants to give an attempt of captivating initiative to get up earlier but she did not put on energy to implement it at least a day. If she might have tried it priorly then there is no necessity of getting frustration when the alarm rang.

If you fit in to this type of case then you will come to know that any thoughts or notions that we make are effective only when we put on some effort to it. Unless and until we jump working on it, the wish that we had will remain to be an inoperable thought or dead initiative.

"Initiative is only the initial thought that anyone can have but it works only when taken into action or consideration"

Alarm for Ms. B

Ms. B drives to bed at 11.30 PM and sets alarm for 4.30 AM in the next morning. she had a good doze that night without any distractions. Let us just imagine if this alarm does ring and there is a problem with her clock, then what will happen to her schedule or work in the next morning? Can she justify this situation?

Let us see what happened on the next day morning. Ms. B kept alarm for 4.30 AM. she   did not wake up on time because the alarm did not ring. Regrettably, she had missed to appear for the chief meeting that is held at her workplace around 7.00 AM. This is because she woke up only at 7.00 AM and looked into the clock. With a countless shock and tautness, she   rang up to her office and vexed to explain the situation which no one would agree to take or believe. Even though it is factual, no one will be able to accept this type of apologies and grant second chance for this reason. As an observer we could realise one thing that Mr B does not make it deliberately. This doesn't seem like a purposeful error of her when the incident is analysed from the general view. But as a practical learner one should approach this situation in such a way that she should have learnt to clarify her fault of not being mindful towards the meeting. Though the alarm's technical issue of ringing occurred her sub conscious mind should be vigilant to wake her up and push her to attend the meeting. Because the status quo will not be favourable for us all the time. It may also cause some change or even cancellation of a work that would not only affect one individual but the plan of others works as well.

This is a kind of incident that indicates the cause of situational changes for which we must be aware of or else it comes out with outcome twist turns in our life. It is very crucial to be conscious and partake control over our intuitive mind then, that we can manage any type of situations.

"Carelessness should be evaded but never forget to care for your carelessness"

Ms. C and her Comfort:

Ms. C drives to bed at 11.00 PM and keeps alarm at three consecutive timings such as 5.00 AM, 6.00 AM, 7.00 AM. Does she have three unlike schedules at these regular intervals? What is the reason behind these three alarms? Did she wake up for the first, second or the third one?

Let us perceive on the happenings the next day morning. Mr C is in profound sleep and the alarms rings at 5.00 AM. With a gluey smile she turns of the alarm affirming "It's just 5 now" and endures to nap. After an hour the second alarm happening to ring at 6.00 AM., she is still pleased and turns off the alarm and continues to sleep. The last alarm is yet to ring. Do you have any presumption about it? May be this hypothesis is different for you but it is the concrete datum according to my reflection made. Ms. C did not wake up this time because she is adept to the sound of alarm and practiced only to switch off it. It was not an alarm sound at all instead it became the lullaby for her. The definite purpose of having three intervals was to wake up step by step and do the mission on time. But the plan goes useless when it is practically applied.

This incident teaches us with something that wake up cannot be a step-by-step process. It should be a rapid rise that breaks away all the laziness. If we necessitate these countless pauses for a meek alarm then imagine how many intervals, we would require to acclimate any big changes that necessitates for our success. The time that we munch for any rest or leisure defines the comfort zone that we are adapted to. One more weighty thing to note from the attitude of Ms. C is the contentment that she had while turning off alarm each time. It means Ms. C is happy and comfortable with sleep rather than her commitments to wake up. she is just an organizer who strategizes for a lazy failed short cut that will go useless and make her super lazy. If she might have avoided those intervals, at least she must have had a decent sleep without any discontinuity in between. It is almost like self-disturbance made by her to disturb herself. Hence her sleep and wake up was hypothetical at the end. It was just like neither sleeping nor woke up.

"Come out of comfort zone to do your best or just be in comfort zone at rest"

Do not attempt the both at the same time. It is merely unbearable.

It is D for Dedication:

Ms. D goes to bed at 11.00 PM and reserved alarm at 5.00 AM in the next morning. Is it probable for her to wake up if the alarm rings? What might be the reason for her to set an alarm?

Let us look into the incident that transpired the next day. This case is slightly unlike when compared to others. Ms. D awakened before the alarm rings and turned off the alarm. This seemed to be unusual but why did she set the alarm? 1f she is able to wake up on her even timings then what could be the cause concealed behind it. One particular thing is the consciousness and interest that she had in her task on the next morning and the other thing is that Ms. D is extra conscious about the alarm. She had the alarm for her supplementary option. She did not stretch way for any situation that can make her plans corrupt and she is now in safer side without any tautness or regretting thoughts.

This incident is a sample for initiating dedication as we see Ms. D had been twin conscious and so she was able to bring about conditions carefully. Therefore, it comprises presence of mind that she holds even at sleep. This can be possible only when there is firm notice on the road to the work that we fix on the next day. That curiosity to pursue will circulate our thoughts all the night and will remind us to wake up without any alarm.

"Decided to be Dedicated then your Duties are already Done"

Ms. E is still Earlier!

Ms. E drives to bed at 10.00 PM and she never had a habit of setting up any alarm to wake up for the next day. Does this mean that she does not have any work on the next day? Does she have any plan for the next day?

What is the motive in arrears not using the alarm to wake up?

Let us see what happened on the next day. Ms. E gets up early in the morning before the sunrise without the alarm sound. Nobody waked her and she did not think about fixing the alarm. She got up prior by herself as she was super mindful with her routines and so she was able to do it. The reason behind it was the regular habit that she had shadowed for a long period of time had now turned out to be the practice instinctively or without depending on alarm or somebody else.

Ms. E did not have any special work on that particular day and was not committed to any work as well. But she got up earlier and sustained her routine.

This incident paves way for our understanding know that we should be prepared to face the new day by waking up earlier. Because getting up earlier pacts moral behaviors which comprises responsibility, punctuality, perfection, and so on

"Either practice or Habit is always the song of long-lasting performance"

Ms. F is a fair player:

Ms. F does not even own a clock. She is economically weak that she is not able to afford for a clock. Ms. F has to get up earlier to meet her basic needs such as food and shelter. Without clock will she be able to achieve her task? Will she get up next morning on time?

Let us see what happened on the next day morning. Ms. F wakes up early morning without checking out the time in the clock as she never required a clock or a cue because she had the impulse to work in order to meet her daily needs. Some natural indications like sunshine, sound of the birds or animals, morning fresh air was more than enough for her to get up on time. Thus Ms. F had practiced to get up earlier due to her prerequisite for financial development, survival and ambition. Later it turned out to be the automatic programmed activities.

This incident outlines us to distinguish that the hunger or passion towards anything will inevitably wake us with any source or even without source.

"Without thirst there is no use for water"

Similarly, without goal there is no use of life span.

The actual Genius Ms. G:

Ms. G needed clock but never used alarm at all. What might be the motive behind the need of clock but not the alarm?

Let us look into the hypothesis about Ms. G who gives the impression that is dissimilar from all others. Ms. G did not nap throughout the night, she was working eagerly for her ambition. She needed clock in order to have a standard time management and schedules but on no occasion required the alarm because she never had desire to sleep as she sought to accomplish her goal. This is how Ms. G styles revolution when equated to others. To express in one word Ms. G is an all-nighter and she needed clock to calculate the time so that more than clock she was fond of lights to work for the whole night. It is easier to prepare a budget for money but budget for time is actually compulsory to leave behind us the success footprints as it will define the life we lived.

This type of people teaches us the value of time and we get to know the distinctiveness existing in Ms. G and we have no uncertainty about her achievement. She will assuredly hit her goal by exhibiting effort to her maximum.

"All-nighter is always a goal hunter"

"Ms. G"

Ms. G is high-minded and I call her as Ms. Genius because she was unlike from all others. The way of approach and perseverance towards her mission looked-for no reminder and desired no break or pause sandwiched between. Hence in this chapter Ms. G is the lesson and she is the star.

The ordinary situations that we face in our life pacts with many things which comprises our psychological behavior, time, endurance, excellence, uniqueness, charm, charisma, and achievement.

CHAPTER- 6

Working of Motivation

"Scarcity in motivation gives way to self- motivation"

Motivation is the crucial factor for any task or attainment. There are many who blame that they do not have any drive or motivation from their known sphere. Dearth of motivation is considered as the foremost blaming whys and wherefores for the individuals. At the present time students gain motivation from the family, friend and the educational institutions where they are involved. But approximately there are weird facts about motivation and deplorable in many cases. The motivation is given habitually to the highfliers and not to the failed individuals who essentially want it. The achievers are the one who had before now jam-packed their battery with motivation and started working on it. They in point of fact do not need any motivation further as they are quiet on success track running their race. But the failed individuals are the ones who attempt to do something innovative and vision of getting appreciation for their every preliminary effort. They are bursting with disenchantments of failure on the other hand the society liabilities on them for being a looser even putting to death their final drop of self-motivation. Finally, she will come to the verdict that she should halt trying something innovative that will upsurge the fear of self-participation and voluntarily. The society will not motivate her instead it recaps about her incapability, powerlessness, inability and pain of fall that she had earlier.

When you face discrimination, you work hard to prove your worth to that particular person. In the mean time you fail to recall that the one person is the random sample from the whole world. So, you need to stretch your entire efforts to attest to the whole world and not for the individual. Moreover, than proving your strength to the others it is mandate to show yourself who you are as that self-respect will give you the pride and endless happiness

Barriers met due to absence of Motivation:

There are countless disadvantages due to dearth of motivation. They are as follows

1.   The escalation of blaming attitude

One of the riskiest behaviors found in this generation is that their unpaid freelancing occupation is blaming others. This is the easiest way of escaping from the acceptance of one's own mistake. I label it dangerous because it not only affects the individual but also creates disappointments to their surroundings. One scary thing about the blamers is that they can never be contented at any situation and they persist to be the blamers throughout their 1ife. Once this attitude is encouraged it may lead to arrogance and violence which may hurt themselves and their surroundings both physically and psychologically.

"Blamers are the born losers and success is just a dream for them"

## 2.	Cut in Self-esteem

When nobody initiates to appreciate the tiniest efforts of an individual it will assuredly turn out to be a distress. Maybe it is a slightest effort in our point of view but it might be the determined effort taken by that particular individual. If she realizes that it is nothing to be creditable by others then it will indeed create inferiority complex in her and will outcome in under-estimation of her own capacity. But when that individual is given some applause or credits for her work then she will lift up her spirit to do further works. This will be suitable for fearing personality who attempts something innovative to get rid of the distress. Here her cure for all her dread is in the impetus given to her by her family, friends or from her known circles.

"Motivation is the perfect medicine to gain mental strength"

## 3.	Confidence level is being devastated:

Motivation is the only thing that lifts up one's confidence level. It can provoke a fearing one to do any task because motivation delivers confidence and the confidence turns out to be the energy. Such energy is the instantaneous one that can proximately be executed to achieve any task effortlessly. I have stated motivation as the prompt factor because it lasts only for a few widths of time. It is the accountability of the society to renew the energy with the aid of drive. But the actual thing that transpires around us is that the people in the society who are the experts in depicting every single trivial blunder so well without the indication which can even terminate the life of an innocent. This can be linked to the proverb "Bad news travels fast" The gloomy thing to admit here is "No one is good already" and no one has the rights to tell bad about someone without their acquaintance. It can be called as gossiping or being judgmental. Most of the individuals who depend on others and jobless are the best de-motivators. Because they have excess of jealous and anger towards the one who cracks hard to succeed. These insolences will de-motivate the budding effort takers and will easily bring down their confidence level. Once the confidence level comes down it is very problematic to re-build it again.

"The sense of motivation comes from de-motivators whose comments will grant dense of confidence in us"

These are some of the barriers that many of us face day-to-day due to deficiency of motivation and more than enough de –motivation by our closed ones. Let me bounce out some examples for the de-motivation that turned out to be the motivation.

Ms. X is an individual who is remarked, cornered by the people from place to place due to her status, caste, and so on taking advantage of her Introvert Character. Ms. X had no motivation for succeeding her ambition. She ached for appreciation and she exploited so much of her time when days and time overtakes her, she cultivated distress about her ambition. Moreover, she was scared of her surroundings who retain questioning her and finding faults in her every actions. She strained to please them but botched, she strained to impress and amaze them but she remained clown to them, she was earnest to them but she was stabbed, she thought she failed. The failure I meant is only the time and nothing more than that, because she failed to others that is the actually success. Nobody in the world can win to others, since everyone thinks they are superior to others and feel themselves as the special for them. Here the challenge here to win ourselves. Mrs. X in the journey of wining hearts lost herself. She took all her insults as a motivation and she has started writing a book and the book is what you are reading now....

Yes, I grew with inner spirit and thirst to mark that the society is off beam. Hence, I sense I am on track winning people around me and moreover I stopped focusing about people who cursed me, I left them by praying for their disability, their eye sight that is been deficient in seeing positivity in others.

Everybody was in a great shock and Surprise. Many did not believe that they asked many questions to confirm her accomplishment

Yes, as I articulated the society will not be able to be certain of moral things quicker. They always have some qualms before they trust.
This is one of the examples to demonstrate that de-motivation can be taken as the optimistic vibes that tinkle us to work on our goals. So that the outcome expanded out through all our hard work and accomplishment will be the answer for all the interrogations and commentaries made by the society.

I would like to state Motivation in a few sentences. This will stretch a vibrant view and understanding when you look into it. They are as follows;

Say to others "Yes, you can"
Don't hear others "No, you can't"
Others easily accept "Yes, you can't"
Only few motivates "No, you can"

One necessarily should learn to inspire others with the constructive statement "Yes, you can" This will express your charm, feast happiness and creates positive aura to your surroundings. This is the laid-back way of drive but the gloomiest thing is difficultly only few do that.

Do not perceive others de-motivating declarations like "No you can't". This is the utmost habitually overheard statement for all of us. It is recurring frequently by the ones who are very close to us. The adverse statement which can make others dismayed and bounces a lot of deterrence. We must not catch those words or take it utterly and come into inference. Those harmful speeches should be well-thought-out as the dead statement. Because it will not spring life to anybody it can either cause destruction of confidence or ambition.

The thought-provoking thing is others easily agree your failure when you give up and say "No, I can't". The longer you try for your efforts if you fail to get accomplishment faster the criticism for the effort that you take will successfully block you from the triumph. The people around, will look at you and express you that you have untapped your time exhibiting that they feel misfortune for you so easily ending up influencing you to drop the task. Don't ever believe them because they are the one who uses your emotions and insist you to halt your way of success.

Finally, I would like to salute those personalities who says "No, you can" are very rare to the society. They are the authentic motivators. When we are so distraught and exhausted, we usually give up but they are the one who galvanize, power up the batteries to our feelings and idea with the impetus. The most apt examples for this category could be the parents especially Mother. If you have someone exceptional apart from parents and teachers then they are certainly genuine and awesome motivators who has the capability to impart good things and banquet constructive vibes around the society.

Hence Motivation is a moral factor that can root moral changes in life of many individuals.

CHAPTER-7

Thirst

"The thirst of water will bring you out of the desert"

Similarly, the thirst of work will crop you to efficacious future. May be this day, time, the age you are in might seem to be a desert but it will not endure for an elongated time if you travel without a pause, you can come out of it earlier. It is obligatory to shoot some questions to all. The interrogations are as follows:

What is the idea about the work you choose?

"Choose it not if you have idea to pause it, yes"

The work you pick to do necessarily should be collaborative with your interest and your talent. Earning Money must not be the initial cause to do any work. The toil you go through should not benefit only you selfishly, it ought to advantage your surroundings in as well.

What could be the responsibility of your work?

"In charge of the work you take
Charge you earn is not enough to make

For it is to just a wake
To pursue your purpose"

The responsibility of the work is in the mode of doing it. That is the earnestness and the influence that you brand for the pay that you get for it. Thus, one must suit up to her responsibility and start working on it.

What is working?

"Be it a real king
Cannot be it if, not working"

I would like to outline WorKING as "We are the KING". We may be the workforces, labors or the staffs to our owners but we are the KING to ourselves and to the people around us when we work. Working makes us to be an independent individual who can manage themselves without being liable on others economically. It does not matter about the kind of work you do or the designation. It is nothing much deferrable between the work with minimum pay and the work that pays you high. Working delivers dignity, self-respect, contentment and self-satisfaction to all. Many in this world could be multi-millionaires but still they prioritize it with schedules because they knew that happiness does not come from money alone it includes self-satisfaction, dignity etc... Happiness comes from the work that we contribute to earn money. Doing numerous works stretches physical pain on one side but work is the only mental strength for human to survival. It provides confidence for the individual to face her life by himself.

"A working hand can even understand the ache of the sand in the land"

Understanding is the key of all moral behaviors. Working individual can with no trouble comprehend the agony of anybody or anything It might be the other living beings that slog day and night like nature which makes us to live healthy. The hard worker can find the wow in any source that she gets she will not ever be a blaming person because she makes every catastrophe as her lesson for her further accomplishments. she learns from her mistakes and earns out of her success. Therefore, she is able to differentiate the sources that root good and bad situations in her life. She can neither be a looser nor a failure in her life. She is always an achiever, a daily high-flier who does farm duties on daily basis and runs her life and takes care of her family without any crisis she hides all the pain inside and spends happy time with her beloved ones and well-wishers.

The sacrifice that every working hands make are uncountable and not considerable as sand. The sand only knows the pain that it has while we walk on it. Similarly, the pain in working hand is multiple but it invisible and inconsiderable as sand particles.

*"To pay bill for things you purchase
I say race to chase and face things"*

This is all about a working hand which could give you to have thirst for work.

CHAPTER-8

Ideas about Idea

"Morning cannot wake you up. But Ideas can do"

Obviously, it is true that Ideas can wake you up not from the night sleep but from the day dreams. Because ideas do not let you sleep it helps you to work on it. Idea comes out of deep thinking and creativity. Everyone is a creator of new ideas it might be exhibited by the way of speaking, style, attitude, behavior. Many of us do not realize that in every activity we do there are some ideas hidden. It might be a silly idea but still it might have been worked out so well after implementation. The best example of exhibiting ideas started through speaking especially during the fun made to make others laugh. Thus, the creativity was initially used to entertain others by spilling out funny words and funny actions that were made to make others happy. Every idea that succeeded might have been implemented with the purpose of making others happy. Many ideas became dangerous when it had the purpose of making impossible things happen. Mostly scientists were affected due to implementation of idea to find new things. Scientist had made some assumptions to create new things and this happens due to greediness of human. The competitions we face between countries makes us to create new things. Some of the ideas gave many inventions which was useless to the world. Even though it was useless the world praised it because it was innovative and different.

Later on, business and marketing evolved to sell the invented products by creating brands for everything. We all know that marketing exists mainly for luxury and unnecessary products that we already have. The inventors alliterate some features and double the cost and we still knew it and buy it. A good that is sold out without marketing can only be considered as the essential or potential discovery or idea and it emerges only for a few individuals.

"When you see what no one sees then you are a finder you will be called as the fine find one day"

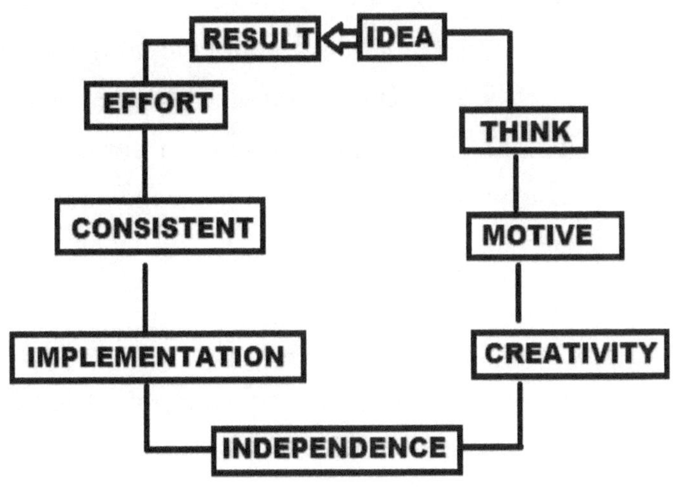

Launch of Idea is the commencement that travels through time and process to attain the destination or result or success. In the journey of accomplishment never think about possibility or probability and halt working as they are the barriers that occurs in any environment. Believe in what you can.

No difference I find between Result and success as both are destiny of the hard work.

See things carefully because a finder can analyze something that is even not even visible to our naked eyes. Yes, the greatest example is finding of various bacteria's that is not visible to our eyes happened due to the discovery of microscope. This was considered to be useful because it helps to find various other harmful that are harmful to human health There is no selfishness or money mindedness while bringing out such ideas. On the other hand, the discovery of solar system and planets, travelling to moon are some of the ideas that came out of selfishness and competition between countries in order to exhibit the pride of the nation.

Ideas have both pros and cons in our life. It may turn out to be the boon when the purpose is good and equal effort is taken earnestly towards it. It may result as a curse when greediness becomes the root cause of the idea.

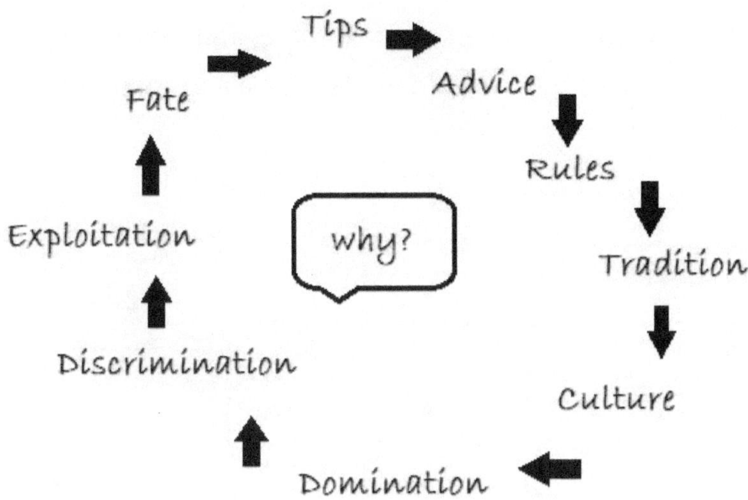

Why to upkeep all these stuffs?

Why to let the tips from the Society decide your Fate of life?

Whatever is forced from the external forces cannot influence you but can put your life into stress, so it is okay to make slipups and learn from it rather than being perfect and woe to satisfy the society who had already designed your fate "STRESS"

"Stay Deaf it is easier, because we have already been practiced to be dumb"

It is not because of the coercion the women shadow all the tradition and culture stuffs. It is in the demand of care, protection and beyond all the Fear of losing her beloved makes a women addictive, slave or clown when the other one doesn't bother about these sacrifices. She drops hope in humanity, love, care and finally the fear of holding someone is replaced with the fear of loving someone.

Life desires assorted emotions to live it and it is easy if no one hinders to spoil the flow. Believe in others kindness if seems to be true but not the wrong influencers. It is difficult to do it but when you have strong emotions and love for yourself then you will not be trapped. Have no emotions to people, as once if they forcefully opinionating on you then it is sure that they have at least a benefit out of it. One life we have and is the only property we have. Wake up and live it as your wish, without hurting, ruling and cheating others. In this cycle I haven't mentioned about success as I feel living the life with all these is itself a success.

"Anything you do shouldn't harm your surroundings". Holding this one principle, go for any extreme to live your life with purpose that your heart decides so that you don't regret at the end.

I label you as My Beautiful., But when you wish to describe yourself make sure you are "Indescribable" so that you don't change yourself for others expressive and praising passing clouds words.

I hope after reading this book you get certain idea about life, about the surroundings, about the society and about all the unwanted stuffs around. But if you find your stuff and stop concentrating about all about others, you will love every characteristic about you Interesting and live with it and for it.

"Remember" you are born to be happy it is just the bad memories that you were a part of and the wrong options that you have selected altered your situations. But in any Situation, you can win.

With the simple Idea
"Be you" ...

See you!